STRAIGHT TALK

Drugs and Alcohol

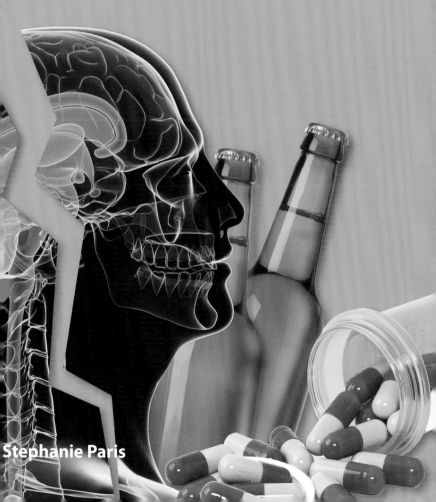

Stephanie Paris

Consultants

Timothy Rasinski, Ph.D.
Kent State University

Lori Oczkus
Literacy Consultant

Dana Lambrose, M.S.N., PMHNP
West Coast University

Based on writing from
TIME For Kids. TIME For Kids and the *TIME For Kids* logo are registered trademarks of TIME Inc. Used under license.

Publishing Credits

Dona Herweck Rice, *Editor-in-Chief*
Lee Aucoin, *Creative Director*
Jamey Acosta, *Senior Editor*
Lexa Hoang, *Designer*
Stephanie Reid, *Photo Editor*
Rachelle Cracchiolo, *M.S.Ed., Publisher*

Image Credits: pp.8–9, 14 Alamy; p.38 Corbis; p.11 FDA; p.27 (middle) DeAgostini/ Getty Images; p.13 (top) iStockphoto; p.23 The Library of Congress [LC-USZ62-123257]; pp.20–21, 25, 30–31 Timothy J. Bradley; All other images from Shutterstock.

Teacher Created Materials
5301 Oceanus Drive
Huntington Beach, CA 92649-1030
http://www.tcmpub.com
ISBN 978-1-4333-4859-4
© 2013 Teacher Created Materials, Inc.

Table of Contents

What Are Drugs?

People talk a lot about drugs. But what they say may not always make sense. You may hear there was a drug bust on the news. Or you may hear about someone who is having trouble with drugs. But there is also a drugstore on the corner. You may hear about people being in **rehab** because they are drug **addicts**. But maybe you know someone who needs to take drugs to stay alive. How can they all be talking about the same thing?

Some drugs are legal, and some are illegal. Some drugs are medicines that can be helpful to your body. They can be used to treat illnesses. Others only cause harm. So when people talk about drugs, they may be talking about many different things.

A drug is any substance—other than food or water—that changes the way your body or mind works.

THINK LINK

1 What questions do you have about drugs?

2 Why do you think it is difficult for some people to talk about drugs?

3 How can you make healthy choices for your body?

5

Addiction

One word that comes up a lot when talking about drugs is **addiction**. Being addicted to something means it is really difficult to stop using it. A person's body and brain get tricked into thinking the drug is needed to feel good. Addicts may understand that something is causing them harm. But they still feel unable to stop. Addiction is very complicated. And it isn't something that can be faced alone.

Withdrawal

If someone stops taking drugs, he or she can feel very sick. It may be weeks before the drugs are completely out of the body. Someone who stops taking drugs may throw up, shake, or sweat a lot during **withdrawal**. Withdrawal is a physical and emotional reaction. It lasts until the person gets used to not having the drug again.

STOP the CYCLE

Drugs are chemicals. They change the way the brain normally works. Over time, people can develop a **tolerance** to drugs. They find they need to take more and more just to feel the same way.

SIGNS of ADDICTION

Addicts may behave in different ways. These are some of the signs of addiction.

spending more and more time and energy on getting and using the drug

doing things you don't usually do (like stealing) to get the drug

feeling that you need the drug to deal with your problem

66 **The chains of habit are generally too small to be felt until they are too strong to be broken.** 99
—Samuel Johnson, poet

keeping an extra amount of the drug on hand

spending money you can't afford on the drug

failing to stop using the drug when you try

believing that you need to use the drug regularly

Types of Drugs

There are many kinds of drugs. They can be divided into groups based on how they are used, what form they come in, and what effects they cause.

Prescription Drugs

A **prescription** is a note from a doctor that says someone needs a specific medicine. Doctors need to know the patient's age and weight when they write prescriptions. They also need to know if the patient is taking other drugs. This is because many drugs **interact** in negative ways. Something that is safe on its own may be dangerous if another drug is in the body. Medicines are matched to patients and their current needs. It is important to take the right amount and follow the directions. If there are any problems, the doctor needs to be informed.

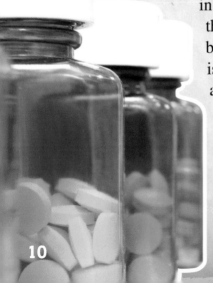

READING a PRESCRIPTION

Rx stands for the Latin word *recipere* or *recipe*, meaning "you take." Prescriptions used to be recipes telling the pharmacist how much of each medicine to put in.

R
X DOCTOR _____
ADDRESS _____
TELEPHONE _____

DATE : __/__/__

PATIENT'S NAME _____
ADDRESS _____

MEDICINE _____

DOCTOR'S SIGNATURE _____

FULL APPROVAL

Every prescription drug goes through a long process before it is approved. In the United States, the Food and Drug Administration (FDA) is in charge. It makes sure that prescription drugs are safe when used as directed.

Prescription Abuse

Sometimes people **abuse** drugs by taking them in ways that differ from the prescription. They might think prescription drugs are safe because they came from a doctor. People may take too much of the medicine. Or they may take drugs that were prescribed for other people. This is very dangerous! Each prescription is different and has its own risks. Many can make you sick if you take too much. Some can be dangerous if taken with alcohol or mixed with other things. Some can kill you. In 2008 alone, 20,044 deaths were caused by taking prescription drugs in amounts greater than the prescribed **dose**.

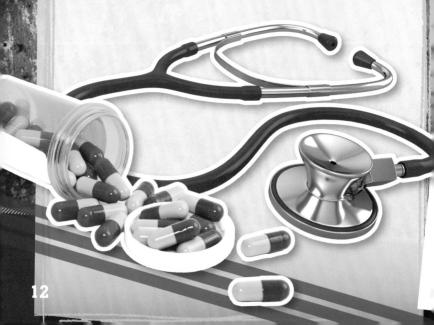

More people in the United States die from prescription drug abuse than from **heroin** and cocaine combined!

DOCTOR'S ORDERS

It's important to know your body, but remember, only a doctor should advise you on what drugs to take. **Self-medicating** with prescription drugs is dangerous.

Warning

Most medicines come with a piece of paper. It may look small, but when unfolded, it becomes a long sheet filled with small writing. This pamphlet tells about all the side effects and possible problems that can happen with the drug. Most medicines are safe when taken as directed. But if taken in other ways, medicines can cause problems.

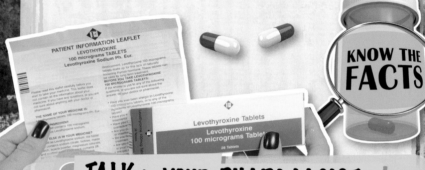

TALK to YOUR PHARMACIST

Pharmacists are specially trained to dispense prescription medication to patients. They can also explain doctors' instructions and possible side effects so medications can be taken safely and effectively. Be sure to talk to your pharmacist if you have any questions about your prescription.

Think only a certain type of person becomes an addict? Think again. Addiction can affect anyone regardless of age, gender, ethnicity, intelligence, or wealth.

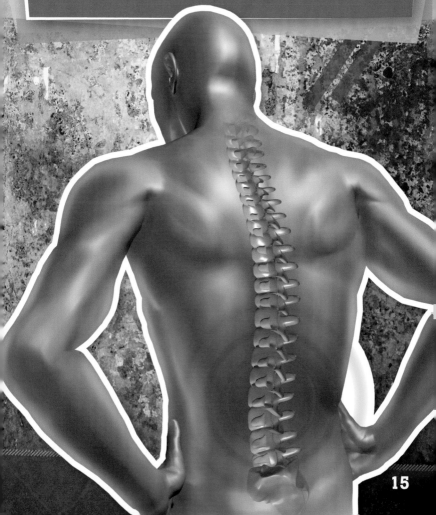

NARCOTICS

Narcotic pain pills are the most abused prescription drugs. They are also among the deadliest. Some people feel relaxed and happy when they take them. So, they may take them when they don't need to. Narcotics are made from the same plant as heroin. They are very addictive! When abused, they can make people stop breathing. If taken with alcohol or other drugs, the risks are even greater.

15

Illegal Drugs

Illegal drugs are those that are against the law to use or sell. Cocaine, heroin, LSD, crystal meth, and Ecstasy are all illegal. Marijuana is illegal in most parts of the world. But some places allow doctors to prescribe it to adults with certain illnesses, such as cancer.

One of the reasons these drugs are illegal is that they can be dangerous. They can hurt your heart, lungs, and **nervous system**. And when people are taking these drugs, they don't make good choices. They have a hard time thinking clearly. They may even choose to do dangerous things that can cause harm to themselves or others.

marijuana plant

The FIRST ILLEGAL DRUG

In 1875, San Francisco passed the first anti-drug law. It was made to fight the problem of opium addiction. Opium is the main ingredient found in heroin.

UPS and DOWNS

One way drugs are grouped is by what they do and how they make people feel.

Depressants

These make people feel less alert. They slow activity in the brain. Alcohol is a **depressant**.

Stimulants

These make people feel more energetic. Caffeine is a legal **stimulant**. Crystal meth is an illegal one.

Hallucinogens

These drugs make people see or hear things that aren't there. LSD and some mushrooms are **hallucinogens**.

Narcotics

These drugs dull people's senses and lessen pain. They can also make people sleepy. Prescription painkillers, like oxycontin, are legal narcotics. Others, like heroin, are illegal.

High Costs

To **overdose** means to take so much of a drug that it could lead to death. For illegal drugs, the amount it takes to overdose varies. Prescription drug makers have very strict rules to ensure that each dose has an exact amount of the drug in it. Illegal drug makers don't follow any rules. Because of this, it's hard to know how a drug will affect each person. One time, the drug may be weak. The next time, it may be strong. In fact, it could be so strong that a single dose could lead to an overdose!

COCAINE

Cocaine is a stimulant. It can make people feel very energetic, as if they could do anything. But, that is just when they are on the drug. Later, they may feel sad and scared. Cocaine is very addictive. And, it has another problem. It can cause heart attacks—even in kids and teenagers.

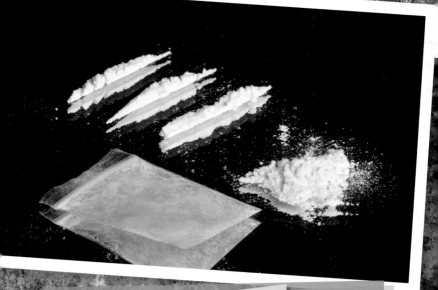

DRUG SLANG

Many drugs go by different names. Sometimes, people try to make the names sound cute or cool. Cocaine may be called *blow*, *rock*, or even *nose candy*. The people who sell and use the drugs want them to sound fun and inviting.

ANATOMY of an OVERDOSE

Taking too much of any drug—even a drug that's normally safe—can cause a dangerous overdose. These are the symptoms to watch for.

difficulty moving

strange moods

sweating

Note: It is always best to call 911 right away if you think someone is experiencing an overdose or alcohol poisoning.

Don't be afraid of getting in trouble. You'll feel worse if someone dies.

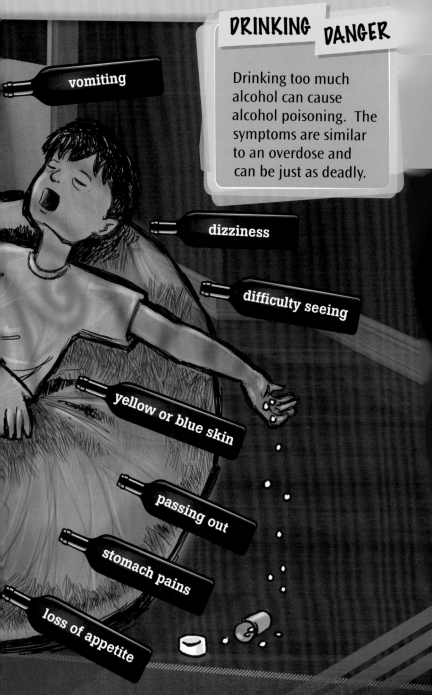

DRINKING DANGER

Drinking too much alcohol can cause alcohol poisoning. The symptoms are similar to an overdose and can be just as deadly.

vomiting

dizziness

difficulty seeing

yellow or blue skin

passing out

stomach pains

loss of appetite

21

Alcohol

Alcohol is a legal drug. It is a chemical that is made when natural sugars **ferment**. Beer and wine have some alcohol in them. Drinks like vodka, gin, bourbon, and tequila have more. None of these drinks are safe for kids. This is because kids' bodies are still growing. Adults can choose to drink alcohol. But too much is not good for anyone. **Alcoholics** are people who are addicted to alcohol.

PROHIBITION

Alcohol was once illegal in the United States. In January 1920, the 18th Amendment to the Constitution was passed. This law made it illegal to sell or transport alcoholic drinks in the United States. This time period was known as **Prohibition** because people were prohibited, or stopped, from getting alcohol.

Prohibitionists dump alcohol as police watch.

The 21st AMENDMENT

Just 13 years after Prohibition started, the United States passed a new law. The 21st Amendment ended Prohibition.

LEGAL DRINKING AGES AROUND the WORLD

In the United States, people are allowed to drink alcohol after turning 21. In other countries, the legal drinking age is lower. But people who start drinking when they are 15 are 4 times more likely to become alcoholics than people who don't drink until they are 21. The earlier people begin drinking, the more likely they are to become addicted later in life.

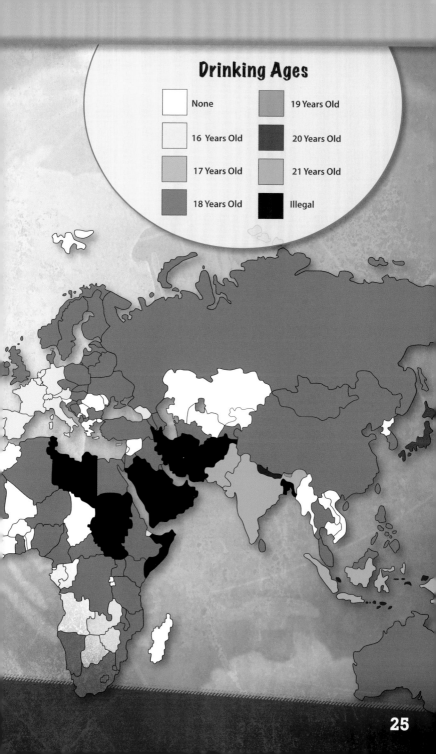

Drinking Ages

None	19 Years Old
16 Years Old	20 Years Old
17 Years Old	21 Years Old
18 Years Old	Illegal

Alcohol and the Body

Alcohol is a depressant. So it slows down the nervous system. It makes it harder to stay in control and make good decisions. Alcohol makes people act and think differently than they normally would. They may be silly and happy one minute. But they may be sad or angry the next moment. They may have trouble walking or talking. And they may do things they regret.

Too much alcohol is poisonous. It can make people so sick they throw up or **pass out**. Or it can kill them. Alcohol can hurt people's bodies over time, too. It can cause heart and nerve damage. And alcohol is extremely bad for the liver, which filters out poisons.

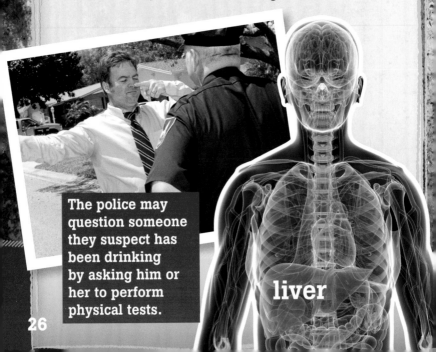

The police may question someone they suspect has been drinking by asking him or her to perform physical tests.

liver

EARLIEST ALCOHOL

The earliest known alcoholic beverage dates back to about 7,000 BC in China. It was a mixture of fermented rice, honey, and hawthorn fruit or grapes.

ANCIENT EGYPTIAN BEER

In ancient Egypt, people drank a sweet beer made from bread. It didn't have very much alcohol. And it was so thick people needed to use a special straw to drink it.

STAYING HEALTHY

Many historians believe that much of the fresh water in the ancient world had so many germs in it that it would make people sick. Alcohol kills germs. So in ancient times, drinking wine or beer (with only a little alcohol in it) may have been safer than drinking water!

27

How to Handle It

By now it should be clear that abusing drugs and alcohol is very dangerous. So, why do people do it? What can you say if someone is pressuring you? What are some fun things you can do instead? And what should you do if you or someone you know needs help?

Why People Use Drugs

Sometimes, people like the way drugs make them feel. People who feel sad or upset may hope drugs will let them escape those feelings for a while. But the drugs don't solve the problems. In fact, they usually cause many more problems. And the bad feelings come back when the drugs wear off.

Peer Pressure

Sometimes, people try using alcohol or other drugs because they want to impress their friends. They may think it will make them look cool. Sometimes, you may see people on TV or in movies using drugs. Popular kids may talk about alcohol or drugs. It may seem like everyone is doing it. But that is NOT true.

Only one in six people who need drug treatment in America get it.

RECOGNIZING PEER PRESSURE

Peer pressure takes many forms. Recognizing it is the first step to resisting peer pressure.

Unspoken Pressure

Reasoning

"Just a little won't hurt."

STOP! THINK...

- How do you feel when someone tries to pressure you to do something?

- What form of pressure do you think is hardest to recognize?

- What are some ways to handle peer pressure?

Rejection

"I'm leaving if you won't try it."

Put-Downs

"Don't be a loser. Just try it."

Saying No

Sometimes, people are afraid that refusing to drink or use drugs will make them look bad in front of their friends. But true friends won't want you to do something that makes you uncomfortable. They will understand. But, it is still nice to have some ideas about what you might say if someone offers you drugs or alcohol.

IN YOUR OWN WORDS

Here are a few lines that have worked for other people.

- ➤ No, thanks.
- ➤ No, I'm not into that.
- ➤ Nah, man. I'm OK, thanks.
- ➤ No! If my mom found out I would totally be in trouble!
- ➤ I'm on the _____ team, and I don't want to risk it. They do drug testing at my school. I might get caught and kicked off the team.
- ➤ No, I don't know what that pill could do to me.
- ➤ Nah, that stuff can kill you. Forget it!
- ➤ Nah, let's go (to the mall, to my house to watch a movie, skateboarding, play video games, etc.) instead.
- ➤ That's a terrible idea. I am outta here.
- ➤ I'm going to go _____. You can come if you want to.
- ➤ A friend of mine got into that stuff, and it was really horrible.
- ➤ Nah, I really don't like how it makes people act.

These are just some suggestions of the kinds of things you can say. But if this isn't how you talk, you should say it in your own way.

A Better Party

Sometimes, people have a hard time turning down drugs because they think they need them to have a good time. But that isn't true. When people are using drugs, they aren't really themselves. So they can't truly enjoy what they are doing. Luckily, all it takes to "party" is having a good time with friends! And the best friends are those who don't pressure you to use drugs.

Life is an adventure. The future holds fun surprises. There may also be challenges ahead. Issues at school or at home can be upsetting. But good friends make it easier. And being healthy makes it easier, too. Playing sports, making art, writing, or spending time outside are all good ways to blow off steam. And all these activities are easier to enjoy when you're **sober**.

PARTY ON!

What are some other ways that you could make a party fun? What other sorts of things do you like doing with your friends?

DRUGS GET in the WAY

Sometimes, people use drugs and alcohol because they think they will help them relax or take their mind off their worries. The truth is that when the good feelings wear off, drugs make our lives more stressful. There are so many easier and safer ways to relax and have fun. And there's always something new to try.

If you want to relax,

try yoga, listening to music, or talking with a friend.

If you want to challenge yourself,

take an advanced class in your favorite subject. Or try running a race!

If you want to express yourself,

draw a comic book or write a story about your life.

TAKE the CHALLENGE

At the website abovetheinfluence.com, different kids from across the country share ways they spent their weekends without wasting them on drugs. See if you can come up with ways to have an "unwasted weekend!"

Risks to Others

One of the biggest problems with drugs and alcohol is that they don't just hurt the person taking them. When people are on drugs, they may act recklessly. They may make decisions that hurt the people around them. They may try to drive. Driving under the influence of drugs or alcohol is a bad decision. It puts the driver and others in danger. Drugs and alcohol can cause people to do things they wouldn't usually do. They may even steal or get violent.

Getting Help

If you think that you or someone you know has a problem with alcohol or other drugs, you need to get help. It's best to talk with a trusted adult. This might be your mom or dad, another family member, a school counselor, or someone at your church. An adult can find the right kind of help for you.

CONSEQUENCES

Besides the danger to your health, drugs and alcohol can lead to many other bad consequences:

> Expulsion from school
> Large fines
> Jail time/juvenile hall
> Loss or suspension of driver's license
> Loss of vehicle
> Fewer job options

DEADLY STATS

Car crashes are the leading cause of death among young people ages 15 to 20. Each year, nearly 2,000 people under age 21 die from car crashes that involve underage drinking.

People who are addicted to alcohol or other drugs need help. But if they get help, they can stop using them.

What to Remember

It's normal to be curious about drugs. This book is one way to get some of the answers. But there are many others. Trusted adults are the best way. They can help you find answers to any other questions you have.

There may always be pressure to drink and try drugs. But when you know the risks, you can make smart choices. You can decide what's important in your life. You have the power.

DRUG FREE SCHOOL ZONE

Glossary

abuse—using a drug in a way that isn't safe or recommended by a doctor

addiction—a strong and harmful need to regularly have something

addicts—people who are unable to stop using drugs or alcohol

alcoholics—people who are addicted to alcohol

cocaine—a powerful drug

depressant—a drug that slows down the brain and nervous system

dose—a measured amount of a medicine to be taken at one time

ferment—to change sugars into alcohol

hallucinogens—substances that make you experience something that is not real, like a waking dream

heroin—a drug made from morphine

illegal drugs—drugs that are against the law to use or sell

interact—when one substance changes how another substance acts

narcotics—drugs that dull pain and make people drowsy

nervous system—the system that sends signals between the brain and the body

overdose—taking so much of a drug that it's harmful

pass out—to lose consciousness or mental awareness

prescription—a doctor's note describing what medicine to take and how much of it to take

Prohibition—the time period from 1920 to 1933 in the United States when alcohol was illegal

rehab—a rehabilitation program that helps someone get over a problem and become healthy again

self-medicating—the process of trying to relieve pain or symptoms without consulting a doctor

sober—not drunk or under the influence of drugs

stimulant—a drug that makes the heart beat faster and makes people feel like they have more energy

tolerance—the ability to adjust to a drug so the effects are experienced less strongly

withdrawal—the symptoms people feel when they try to stop taking a substance to which they are addicted

Index

Bibliography

Jankowski, Connie. *Investigating the Human Body: Life Science (Science Readers).* **Teacher Created Materials Publishing, 2008.**

Discover more about how the body's systems work together and why you should keep your body healthy.

Klosterman, Lorrie. *The Facts about Drugs and the Body.* **Benchmark Books, 2007.**

This book discusses the effects that different drugs have on different parts of the body.

Macaulay, David. *The Way We Work.* **Houghton Mifflin Books, 2008.**

This book gives a colorful close-up look at the way our lungs and heart work. Learn exactly what and how organs are damaged by using drugs.

MacGregor, Cynthia. *Think for Yourself: A Kid's Guide to Solving Life's Dilemmas and Other Sticky Problems.* **Lobster Press, 2008.**

This book is a collection of short passages to help guide you in solving life's dilemmas.

Sommers, Annie Leah. *College Athletics: Steroids and Supplement Abuse (Disgraced! The Dirty History of Performance-Enhancing Drugs in Sports).* **Rosen Publishing Group, 2009.**

This book covers corrupt practices and drug use in college athletics and the effects of illegal drug use.

More to Explore

Abovetheinfluence.com
http://www.abovetheinfluence.com

Join kids just like you and live above the influence of drugs and alcohol. Here, you will learn the facts about drugs, why people use them, how to help a friend who may be using drugs and/or alcohol, and more.

The Cool Spot
http://www.thecoolspot.gov

Learn the dangers of alcohol and ways to resist peer pressure.

PBS Kids: It's My Life
http://www.pbskids.org/itsmylife/body

On the left, click on *Offline Activities* to access journal pages, conversation starters, and book list. In the middle, under *More Topics*, choose *Drug Abuse* to access information on different drugs, rumors and myths, how to make a difference, and more.

KidsHealth
http://www.kidshealth.org

This website has separate sections for parents, kids, teens, and educators. Movies, games, recipes, and medical dictionaries cover various body-related topics. In the search bar, enter *drugs* for topic-related choices.

Neuroscience For Kids: Alcohol
http://faculty.washington.edu/chudler/alco.html

This website has diagrams and lists that show the effects of alcohol on the different body parts and systems. Find out what happens to children who are subjected to alcohol before they are born.

About the Author

Stephanie Paris is a seventh generation Californian. She has her Bachelor of Arts degree in psychology from the University of California, Santa Cruz, and her multiple-subject teaching credential from California State University, San Jose. She has been an elementary classroom teacher, an elementary school computer and technology teacher, a home-schooling mother, an educational activist, an educational author, a web designer, a blogger, and a Girl Scout leader. She lives a clean and drug-free life in Germany.